THE PATHWAY TO WEALTH FOR YOUNGSTERS

Unlock the Secrets to Financial Success

A Guide that equips you with the knowledge and tools needed to pave your pathway to financial prosperity.

Adefunke Odumosu (PhD)

Dedication

To the Young Minds Paving the Path to Prosperity

This book is dedicated to the ambitious and determined youngsters embarking on the exciting journey toward financial success. May these pages serve as your compass, guiding you through the pathways of wealth creation and financial empowerment. Your aspirations and commitment inspire the wisdom within these words. May you navigate the world of finance with confidence and resilience, turning dreams into tangible realities.

With admiration and encouragement,

Adefunke Adetutu Odumosu (PhD)

Table of Content

Foreword

It is with great pleasure and anticipation that I introduce the insightful and empowering work, "The Pathway to Wealth for Youngsters." In today's rapidly evolving world, equipping our youth with the knowledge and skills to navigate the financial landscape is more crucial than ever.

Authored by Adefunke Odumosu (PhD), this book serves as a beacon, guiding young minds on a journey toward financial literacy and prosperity. As Vice-Chancellor, I understand the importance of nurturing holistic education, and this book aligns perfectly with that vision. It goes beyond traditional academia, delving into the practical aspects of financial well-being that are often overlooked in formal education.

"The Pathway to Wealth for Youngsters" is not just a book; it's a roadmap for the next generation to forge a secure and successful future. It provides invaluable insights into budgeting, saving, investing, and cultivating healthy financial habits – skills that are instrumental in achieving lifelong financial well-being.

I commend Dr. Odumosu for her dedication to empowering our youngsters with the knowledge they need to make informed financial decisions. This book is a testament to her commitment to the holistic development of our youth.

I encourage every student, parent, educator, and policymaker to embrace the wisdom within these pages. By doing so, we collectively invest in a future where financial literacy is not a luxury but a fundamental tool for success.

Prof. B. B. Lafiaji-Okuneye
Vice-Chancellor
Lagos State University of Education
Oto-Ijanikin/Epe,
Lagos State, Nigeria.

Acknowledgements

Writing this book has been a fulfilling journey, and I express my deepest gratitude to those who have contributed to its creation.

First, I am humbled and deeply grateful for the divine guidance that has illuminated every word and idea. To God, the source of all wisdom and inspiration, I offer my profound thanks for providing clarity, strength, and purpose throughout this endeavour. May the wisdom shared within these pages be a testament to the divine abundance that surrounds us, and may it serve as a beacon for the young minds aspiring to navigate their pathway to wealth with integrity and purpose.

I extend my deepest gratitude to my hubby, Revd. Canon Oladele Odumosu, for his invaluable insights and unwavering support throughout the writing process. His encouragement provided valuable perspectives that enriched the overall narrative. His unwavering support has been a constant source of inspiration, making this journey toward creating 'Pathway to Wealth for Youngsters' all the more meaningful.

To my beloved children, Oluwadamilare and Oreoluwa, you are the heartbeat of this endeavour. Your support, curiosity, and boundless potential have infused every page of this book. Your dreams and aspirations are the guiding light, inspiring me to create a pathway to wealth that is not just about financial success but also about empowering the future generation. Thank you for being the source of joy and inspiration in this journey. May the knowledge within these pages contribute to your growth, resilience, and success in navigating the exciting pathways to wealth.

I am indebted to my friends and family for their patience, encouragement, and belief in the importance of empowering the younger generation with financial wisdom. To the young individuals whose stories and aspirations have inspired this work, thank you for being the driving force behind 'Pathway to Wealth for Youngsters.'

Finally, to the readers, may this book be a source of guidance and empowerment on your pathway to financial success.

With sincere gratitude,

Odumosu, Adefunke Adetutu PhD.
Associate Professor of Business Administration (Entrepreneurship),
Department of Business and Entrepreneurship Education,
College of Vocational and Entrepreneurship Education,
Lagos State University of Education,
Oto-Ijanikin/Epe,
Lagos State, Nigeria
odumosuaa@lasued.edu.ng

1.

Introduction

If you don't find a way
to make money
while you sleep,
you will work until
you die.

WARREN BUFFETT

Hey there, Future Money Master!
Welcome! In this book, I will talk about something super important: Money! But don't worry, I'll keep it simple and fun. Money is like a giant puzzle; I'm here to help you combine all the pieces.

You might wonder, "Why do I need to learn about money? I'm still young!" Well, that's a great question! Financial literacy is a fancy way of saying "knowing how to handle money." It's a superpower that can help you in many ways. Why, you ask? Let's dive in and find out.

✔ **You're in the driver's seat:** As you grow up, you'll start making decisions about your money. Whether saving up for something you really want, buying things you need, or planning for your future, you want to make intelligent choices. Financial literacy is your trusted co-pilot, helping you make the best choices.

✔ **Avoiding money pitfalls:** We've all heard stories of people who got into financial trouble. I want to help you avoid those problems so you can avoid those pitfalls. Understanding money now means you'll be ready to handle it wisely as you age.

✔ **Your dreams, your goals:** Money can help you achieve your dreams and goals. Want to travel, start a business, or help others in need? Financial literacy can help you get there faster.

✔ **Independence:** Learning about money gives you a taste of independence. You won't have to rely on others to make financial decisions. Instead, you'll have the knowledge and skills to make the right choices.

✔ **Confidence:** When you know how to manage your money, you'll feel more confident about your future. You'll be able to set goals and make plans, and knowing you're in control of your financial destiny gives you a fantastic feeling.

So, in this book, I'll break down the mysteries of money into simple, easy-to-understand concepts. I'll cover saving, budgeting, investing, and much more.

I'll also share tips, and real-life examples to make your journey into financial literacy exciting and empowering. Are you ready to embark on this adventure and unlock the secrets of financial success? Let's get Started!

2.
Building the Foundation for Wealth: Your Roadmap to Financial Success

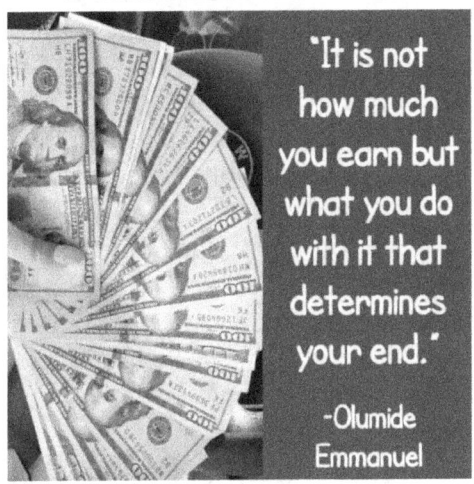

'It is not how much you earn but what you do with it that determines your end."

-Olumide Emmanuel

Hi, Future Money Influencers!

Let's talk about something super important – building the foundation for wealth. It might seem like a big idea, but I'll break it down into simple steps.

☐ Understanding Wealth and Financial Well-being

Have you ever wondered what wealth really means? It's not just about being super rich or having a pile of money; it's about being financially secure and achieving your goals. Imagine being able to cover your basic needs like food, shelter, and school expenses and even some of your wants like a cool new gadget or a fun vacation. It is about having the capacity to fulfill your desires and aspirations; it provides the freedom and opportunity to make choices that align with your goals and dreams.

Now, let's talk about something super important: Financial well-being – The Key to a Happy Life. Financial well-being means having enough money to do what you want while being prepared for unexpected surprises. It's like having a plan for your money so you can live your life comfortably and happily. Financial well-being is not exclusively about the size of one's bank account but also pertains to the financial knowledge, skills, and habits that enable individuals to effectively navigate their financial lives, achieve their financial goals, and experience peace of mind.

☐ Common Misconceptions About Wealth

Misconceptions about wealth are widespread, and setting the record straight is crucial. Here are a few common myths:

> ✔ **Wealth is only for the rich:** Many people believe that only those born into wealthy families or high-paying jobs can become wealthy. Not true! Wealth is not solely reserved for the rich. Anyone can build wealth, no matter their starting point. It's about managing money wisely, saving, investing, and making informed financial decisions.

✔ **You need a lot of money to start building wealth**: Some believe that building wealth requires substantial money. The truth is that you can indeed begin accumulating wealth with small sums of money. The ability to manage what you have, consistent savings, smart choices, and investments can grow your wealth over time.

✔ **Wealth is all about luck:** People often think wealth is primarily a result of luck, such as winning the lottery or inheriting money. Luck can play a role, but it's mostly about making informed choices and responsible financial habits. Hard work, smart financial decisions, and perseverance are key factors.

✔ **You have plenty of time to save:** One common misconception is that young, hardworking individuals may believe they don't need savings, especially if retirement is far off. However, the best advice is to start saving immediately, whether for retirement or other goals like projects or vacations. Starting early is crucial because time is limited, and waiting for a higher income can lead to lifestyle inflation. Even small savings can significantly impact your financial well-being in the long run.

✔ **Debt is normal:** Many individuals mistakenly believe that borrowing or acquiring loans is a common and inconsequential practice. This misconception is particularly harmful as it can severely damage your financial well-being. Developing a habit of purchasing items beyond your means is a sure path to financial disaster. It's vital to resist the temptation to view substantial debts as routine, as doing so will hinder your wealth-building efforts and necessitate the allocation of a significant portion of your resources for debt repayment. Additionally, spending within your financial capabilities is crucial.

✔ **You deserve to buy nice things because you work hard.** This misconception is based on the belief that your hard work and effort justify indulging in expensive or luxurious purchases. It implies that if you've put in long hours and dedicated yourself to your work, you should reward yourself with extravagant items, regardless of the cost. While it's true that hard work deserves recognition and reward, it's essential to strike a balance between enjoying the benefits of your efforts and maintaining financial responsibility. When you decide to give yourself a treat, ensuring that your actions align with your broader financial objectives and preferences is crucial. Practicing mindful spending entails deliberately selecting how you allocate your funds.

✔ **You don't have what it takes to be wealthy:** This misconception stems from self-doubt; some believe they lack the skills or qualities needed to become wealthy. However, the reality is that it's often a lack of motivation, not skills, that hinders their progress. Overcoming this mindset involves embracing uniqueness, utilizing natural skills, and shifting from a negative scarcity mindset to a positive abundance mindset. Building wealth requires hard work, commitment, and an understanding of the potential benefits of dedication, which rich individuals often exhibit compared to those with a more negative mindset.

☐ The Truth About Building Wealth

You may wonder why knowledge about wealth is important. Wealth is like a magical key that can unlock many doors in life. Understanding and managing money wisely puts you on the road to realizing your dreams and goals. Whether traveling the world, starting your dream business, or helping others in need, wealth can make these dreams a reality.

But remember, it's not just about having money; it's about how you use it to build the life you want. And it all begins with understanding what wealth means and how financial well-being can lead you to a brighter future.

So, keep exploring and learning about money because you're on the right track to building wealth and financial well-being. Your financial adventure is just beginning; the best part is that you're in charge!

3.
The Role of Financial Literacy in Your Life: Your Superpower for a Bright Future

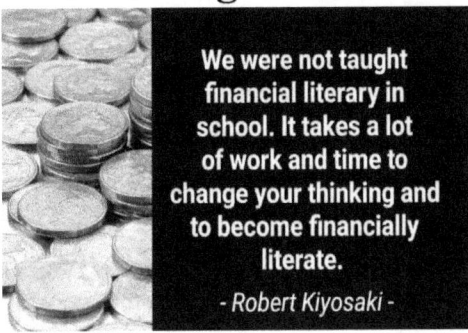

We were not taught financial literary in school. It takes a lot of work and time to change your thinking and to become financially literate.

- Robert Kiyosaki -

Hey there, Young Minds!

Let's talk about something that can be your secret superpower: Financial Literacy. It might not sound thrilling, but trust me, it's like having a superpower that can help you take control of your financial life. I'll explore what it is and why it's so vital for you.

☐ What is Financial Literacy?

Financial literacy is like learning the ABCs of money. It's like learning the rules of a game – the game of managing your finances. It's about understanding how money works, from saving and budgeting to investing and avoiding debt. Your ability to use financial knowledge is your secret weapon for making smart choices with your money.

❑ The Power of Early Financial Literacy

You might think that learning about money can wait until you're older, but starting early is a game-changer. In fact, the financial lessons you learn as a youngster can have a huge impact on your future. Let's explore why and how it can make a real difference in your life.

Early financial literacy helps you:

✔ Cultivate good money habits that can last throughout your lifetime.

✔ Establish a solid foundation that enhances the strength and security of your financial future.

✔ Avoid common financial pitfalls that trip up many adults.

✔ With the knowledge to make informed decisions about spending, saving, and investing, ensuring you are well-prepared for the financial challenges that life may present.

✔ Make the most of your earning potential, even as a youth.

✔ Feel confident and in control of your financial future.

✔ Build a safety net for emergencies, save for future goals, and even invest in growing your money.

Why is Financial Literacy A Superpower?

- ✔ **Making informed choices:** With financial literacy, you're like a financial detective. You can spot good deals, understand bank statements, and make the right choices. It's like having a map that shows you the best route to your financial goals. You'll know how to save, spend, and invest wisely.

- ✔ **Shield against money problems:** It protects against common money problems and unexpected financial storms. You'll learn to steer clear of debt traps and impulse buying, which can drain your finances.

- ✔ **Growing your money:** Financial literacy helps you grow your money into a strong money tree. It's like planting a seed that can turn into a money tree. You'll discover how to save and invest so your money can work for you and grow over time.

- ✔ **Confidence booster:** Financial literacy is like a confidence booster. It empowers you to take control of your financial life and makes you a money expert. You'll feel more capable and less stressed about money matters. This confidence is like a superpower that will serve you throughout your life.

✔ **Money master:** With financial literacy, you become the master of your money. You decide where it goes, what it does, and how it helps you reach your dreams. It's like being the boss of your own financial world.

✔ **Life decisions:** Financial literacy equips you with the knowledge and skills to handle real-life situations that involve money and finances. It helps prepare you for life's big decisions, like buying a car or starting your own business, plan for your future, and navigate various financial challenges and opportunities. It prepares you to face these situations with confidence and competence.

So, remember, financial literacy is your superpower, guide to making wise financial decisions, and your ticket to successfully navigating the world of money. Your financial adventure is just beginning, and with this superpower, you're in control!

4.
Setting Financial Goals: Your Guide to a Brighter Financial Future

Hey, Young Generation!

Let's talk about another important matter – setting financial goals. It might sound a bit grown-up, but it's your roadmap to a brighter financial future. Let's dive into the importance of setting financial goals and how to do it effectively.

☐ The Importance of Setting Financial Goals

Setting goals is like having a treasure map for your money, which is essential for several reasons, especially for youths beginning their journey toward financial independence. Here's why setting financial goals is important

✔ **Give purpose to your money:** When you set financial goals, you're telling your money where to go. This helps you prioritize where your money should go and what it should be used for. Without goals, your money might get spent without a clear plan, making it challenging to achieve what you want.

✔ **Stay focused:** Goals help you stay on track. They give you a reason to save and spend wisely. Instead of spending on random things, you'll focus on your goals.

✔ **Give motivation:** Goals provide motivation and a sense of achievement. When you set specific financial goals, you have something to work towards. Achieving these goals can be rewarding and motivate you to manage your money wisely.

✔ **Budgeting:** It involves monitoring your income and expenses, a crucial step for effective money management and preventing overspending.

✔ **Financial discipline**: Financial goals encourage discipline. It helps you become responsible with your money. When you have a goal in mind, you're less likely to spend impulsively or waste money on things that don't align with your goals. This discipline helps you save and invest more effectively.

- ✔ **Future planning:** Financial goals instill a sense of planning and forward-thinking. Whether it's saving for college, a car, or your first apartment, setting goals helps you plan and allocate resources to achieve these milestones.

- ✔ **Avoiding debt:** Understanding the importance of saving and setting goals can help you avoid falling into the trap of excessive debt, which is a common financial challenge for many young adults.

- ✔ **Financial independence:** Financial goals pave the way for financial independence. This helps you become less reliant on others for your financial needs and gives you control over your money.

- ✔ **Life skills:** Setting financial goals is a valuable life skill that can benefit you as you transition into adulthood. It prepares you for the financial responsibilities you will encounter in college, your first job, and other life stages.

In summary, setting financial goals is critical in managing your finances effectively. It provides direction, motivation, and discipline. It equips you with the essential skills and knowledge to make responsible financial decisions and prepare for your future financial well-being. So, start setting your financial goals today and watch your financial dreams become a reality.

5.
Setting SMART Goals for Building Wealth: Your Simple Guide

Hey, Everyone!

Setting SMART goals for wealth-building is a highly effective approach to ensuring your financial objectives are well-defined and achievable. SMART stands for Specific, Measurable, Attainable, Relevant, and Time-bound. Here's how to apply SMART criteria to your wealth-building goals:

- **Specific:** Your goal should be specific and clear, not vague. Be clear about what you want to achieve.

Ask yourself before setting a goal:

- ✔ What exactly do I want to accomplish?

✔ Why is this goal important?

✔ What are the specific steps I need to take to reach this goal?

For example, instead of saying, "I want to save money," Clearly state what you intend to save for. For instance, "I want to save $500 for a new smartphone."

☐ **Measurable:** Having a measurable goal enables you to monitor your progress and identify when you've accomplished it. It provides a clear benchmark for success.

Pose this question before establishing a goal:

✔ How will I measure my progress?

✔ How will I know when I've reached my goal?

✔ What is the target amount or indicator I'm aiming for?

For example, I will save $50 monthly for ten months to get a new smartphone.

☐ **Attainable**: Your goals should be realistic and achievable. Dream big, but make sure it's something you can do with your current resources. For instance, saving a million dollars by next week might not be achievable.

Before you set a goal, ask yourself:

✔ Is this goal possible for me to achieve?

✔ Do I have the time, knowledge, and resources required?

✔ Are there any obstacles I need to overcome?

For instance, aiming to save $50,000 monthly while working a minimum-wage job may be unrealistic, but setting a more achievable and modest target is advisable.

☐ **Relevant:** Ensure your wealth-building goals matter to you and are relevant to your life and personal aspirations. Don't set goals just because others do. Make sure they align with your values and aspirations.

Ask yourself these questions before you start:

✔ Does this goal align with my long-term financial plan?

✔ Is it meaningful and relevant to my life and values?

✔ Will achieving this goal contribute to my financial well-being?

Your financial goals should make sense in the context of your broader financial strategy.

☐ **Time-bound:** Set a deadline for your goal. A time-bound goal has a precise target date for completion, which creates a sense of urgency and helps you stay focused. It could be by the end of the year, next summer, or any other date that makes sense for your goal.

Question yourself before defining a goal:

- ✔ When do I want to achieve this goal?

- ✔ What can I do daily, weekly, or monthly to reach it on time?

In our example, the goal to save $500 to get a new smartphone could have a time frame like "I will save $500 by the end of ten months by saving $50 every month"

So, in simple terms, SMART goals are like clear targets for your money. They help you stay focused and motivated, making your financial dreams come true. Try setting a SMART goal for something you want to save for and watch your money grow! Your financial adventure is just beginning, and you're in control!

6.
Money Management Essentials: Understanding Income and Expenses

"NEVER SPEND YOUR MONEY BEFORE YOU HAVE IT."

Hi, Potential Financial Luminaries!
Let's talk about something that might sound less exciting but vital: Money Management. Think of it as a critical skill that can unlock doors to your future. Let's break it down in a simple and fun way.

☐ **Understanding Income: Where Money Comes From**

Think of "income" as the money that flows into your wallet. For many youngsters, income can come from various sources:

✔ **Allowances:** Money you receive regularly from your parents or guardians.

✔ **Part-Time Jobs:** Earnings from after-school jobs or gigs.

✔ **Gifts:** Money you get on special occasions like birthdays or holidays.

Understanding your income is essential because it's the starting point for managing your money. It's like the energy you have to fuel your financial journey.

☐ **Identifying Expenses: Where Money Goes**

"Expenses" are like the things that eat up your money. These are the things you spend money on. Your everyday expenses might include:

✔ **Clothing:** The cost of trendy clothes, shoes, and accessories.

✔ **Personal Care:** Expenses for items like skincare products and grooming.

✔ **Entertainment:** Money spent on movies, video games, or hanging out with friends.

Knowing where your money is going is important, just like you'd keep track of your health by monitoring what you eat. Knowing your expenses helps you make smart decisions about your money.

How to Track Your Expenses: A Step-By-Step Guide for Youthful Intellects

Hey guys! Ever wondered how to keep an eye on your spending and become a money-savvy pro? Tracking your expenses is the way to go. It's like having a map for your financial adventure.

Here's how you can do it:

☐ Step 1: Gather Your Tools

Tracking expenses is a crucial aspect of managing your finances. Here are some tools that can help you effectively track your expenses:

- ✔ Tracker Apps like Mint, YNAB (You Need a Budget), and PocketGuard allow you to link your accounts, categorize spending, and set budgets.

- ✔ Spreadsheets like Google Sheets or Excel allow for customization based on your preferences and provide a detailed overview of your spending.

- ✔ Receipt Tracking Apps like Expensify and Receipts by Wave are user-friendly apps that let you capture and categorize receipts on the go.

- ✔ Budgeting Apps like Goodbudget and Wally are for expense tracking, offering insights into your spending habits.

- ✔ Credit Card and Bank Alerts. Set up alert notifications with your credit card or bank to receive notifications for each transaction. This helps you stay aware of your spending in real time.

✔ Digital Wallets like PayPal, Venmo, or Cash App often have transaction history features, allowing you to review your spending patterns.

✔ Manual Tracking using a notebook or journal for those who prefer a hands-on approach to manually recording daily expenses.

✔ Expense Tracking Websites like EveryDollar an online budgeting tool that includes expense tracking features to monitor your spending against your budget.

Choose the tool that aligns with your preferences and habits. Whether you prefer the convenience of mobile apps or the flexibility of spreadsheets, finding the right tool can significantly enhance your ability to manage and control your expenses.

☐ Step 2: Categorize Your Expenses

Organize your expenses into categories to make tracking easier.

Here are some common categories:

✔ **Food:** Think of all the money you spend on snacks, eating out and groceries.

✔ **Clothing:** Include expenses for clothes, shoes, and accessories.

✔ **Personal Care:** Spending on things like skincare products or haircuts.

✔ **Entertainment:** This can include spending on movies, video games, hanging out with friends, or going to an amusement park.

✔ **Savings:** Don't forget to track how much you save. It's like counting your points in a game – every bit counts.

☐ Step 3: Record Your Expenses

Whenever you spend money, it's time to record it:

✔ Keep your receipts when you make a purchase. Write what it was for, like "movie ticket" or "snacks."

✔ If you don't have a receipt, jot down your expenses in a small notebook or use a note-taking app on your smartphone. It's like keeping a journal of your spending adventures.

✔ If you're using a notebook or app, add the expense to the appropriate category.

✔ Don't forget to include the date of the expense. It's like marking your progress in a game.

☐ Step 4: Total It Up

Calculate the total spending within each category at the end of the week or month. It's like calculating your scores in different levels of a game. This gives you a clear picture of where your money is going.

☐ **Step 5: Review and Reflect**

At the end of a week or month, take some time to reflect on your spending. Ask yourself some questions:

- ✔ Are there categories where you spent more than you planned?
- ✔ Are there areas where you can cut back and save more money?
- ✔ Did your spending match your budget, if you have one?

Reflecting on your expenses is like reviewing your gameplay to see how you can improve and become a better player. It's all part of becoming a money-savvy champion.

☐ **Step 6: Stay Consistent**

Just like in your favorite game, practice makes perfect. The more you track your expenses, the better you'll get at it. Over time, it becomes a natural part of managing your money.

So, there you have a step-by-step guide to tracking your expenses. It's your secret weapon for financial success. Keep at it, and you'll be a financial champ in no time!

❑ Here's why tracking your expenses is important:

- ✔ Tracking helps you see where your money is going. It's like shining a flashlight on the hidden spots in a game.

- ✔ When you track your spending, it helps you stay within its limits. You can ensure you're not going over your budget and have enough for everything you need and want.

- ✔ When you track your spending, unexpected expenses won't catch you off guard. It's like seeing obstacles in a game before they trip you up.

- ✔ Tracking your expenses helps you level up your money skills. You become more aware of how you use your money and can make better decisions.

- ✔ Tracking expenses is your secret weapon to reach your financial goals. Knowing where your money goes helps you get there faster. It's like unlocking special achievements in a game.

You'll learn a lot about your spending habits when you track your expenses. You might realize you're spending more on certain things than you thought. It helps you navigate your financial journey, avoid traps, and reach your goals. Get started, and you'll be on your way to becoming a money-savvy champ!

7.
Building Healthy Financial Habits: Savings

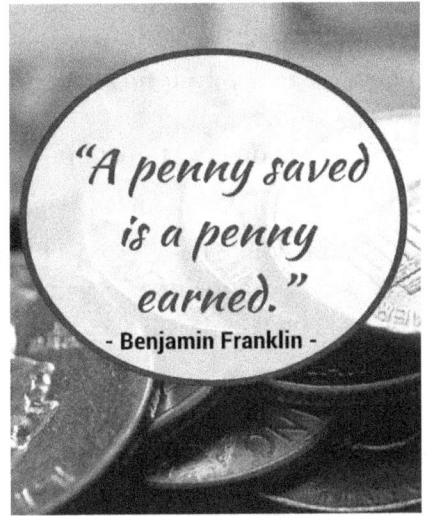

Hello, Aspiring Financial Giants!

Get ready to discover some of the most exciting secrets to building wealth. Building healthy financial habits is like leveling up in a game – it helps you succeed in the real world. This chapter will focus on the topic of savings.

☐ Saving: The First Step to Wealth

Saving money is the very first step on the path to financial success. Let's dive into it in simple language. Imagine you find a shiny coin on the ground. You can keep it in your pocket for later. That's what saving is all about. It's when you take some of your money and keep it safe for the future. When you get money, like your allowance or money from a part-time job, you can decide to keep some of it safe for later.

☐ How to Start Saving: A secret to wealth

Starting to save as an aspiring financial giant can be both fun and rewarding.
Here's a simple guide on how to begin:

- ✔ **Set a goal:** Think about what you want to save for. It could be a short-term goal like buying a new phone or a long-term goal like going to college. Goals keep you focused and motivated.

- ✔ **Create a savings jar or account:** Start by setting up a savings jar or a special savings account at a bank. It's like having a treasure chest to store your money.

- ✔ **Pay yourself first:** Whenever you receive money, like allowance or earnings from a job, put a portion of it into your savings before spending on anything else. It's like rewarding yourself for being a smart saver.

- ✔ **Start small:** You don't have to save much at once. It's a great start, even if it's just a small amount, like a percentage of your allowance or a few dollars. Over time, those small amounts add up.

- ✔ **Automate your savings:** Use technology and its devices to your advantage. You may establish automatic transfers to your savings account to ensure you consistently save without the risk of forgetting. This means that a portion of your money is automatically transferred to your savings account.

✔ **Track Your Progress:** Record how much you save and watch your savings grow. It's like checking your score in a game to see how well you're doing, and this can be super motivating.

✔ **Stay Consistent:** Just like in your favorite video game, practice makes perfect. The more you save, the better you'll become at it. Soon, saving will become a natural part of managing your money.

Remember, starting to save is like embarking on an exciting quest. Each time you save, you get closer to your goals, just as each step takes you closer to winning a game. So, start saving today and enjoy watching your savings grow!

☐ **Saving is essential for these reasons:**

✔ **Emergency fund:** It's like a shield to protect you from unexpected expenses, such as a sudden gadget repair or a medical bill. When you save, you are prepared for unforeseen expenses and won't be surprised.

✔ **Building wealth:** Your savings can grow over time through interest and smart investments. It's like watching your score in a game go up; the more you save, the more it multiplies.

✔ **Goal achievement:** Saving is the key to making your dreams and goals come true, like buying cool gadgets, going to college, or taking that dream vacation.

✔ **Independence:** Saving gives you control over your own money. You won't have to rely on others when you want to buy something or need to take care of yourself.

✔ **Peace of mind:** Knowing you have money saved reduces stress and worry. It's like having a calm and confident character in a video game.

✔ **Opportunity and freedom:** Saving means you're ready to seize exciting opportunities. Whether starting your own business or investing in something you're passionate about, your savings can make it happen.

✔ **Legacy building:** Saving can help you create a financial legacy for your future. You can support your family or causes you care about.

Saving is like planting seeds in a garden. Over time, those seeds grow into big, valuable plants (more money!). So, every bit you save helps you get closer to your dreams. So, start saving today and enjoy these fantastic benefits!

8.
Building Healthy Financial Habits: Budgeting

BUDGET

1.
2.
3.
4.
5.

Budgeting has only one rule: Do not go over budget.

Hi! Future Money-Makers!

In chapter seven, I discussed savings as a critical secret to wealth building. Now, let's delve into budgeting as another component of cultivating healthy financial habits.

☐ Creating a Budget: Your Guide to Managing Money

I'll unravel the mysteries of budgeting in a way that's easy to understand and apply to your everyday life. Budgeting might sound boring, but it is like having a game plan. It helps you ensure you have enough for what you need and want.

Here's how to create a budget that's perfect for a future money-maker like you:

- ✔ **Calculate your income:** You will calculate your total income, like your allowance, money from a part-time job, or gifts every month.

- ✔ **List your expenses:** Draw up a list of everything you spend money on monthly. Divide them into two categories:

  - ▪ **Needs:** These are the things that are essential for your survival and well-being. Without them, it would be tough to live a healthy life. Think of them as the basics you can't do without. Examples are food, clothing, shelter, education, and health care.

  - ▪ **Wants:** These are the things you'd like to have, but they're not necessary for survival. They are based on your preferences, desires, and what makes you happy. Examples are video games, going to the movies, fancy clothes, travel, adventures, and gadgets like smartphones and tablets.

    Note: On your list, needs should always come first, while wants come after needs. Want is like bonus points or rewards in a game; you can aim for them once you've met your needs. Distinguishing between needs and wants helps you make smart decisions about using your money. It's like making choices in a game; you prioritize the important tasks first and then enjoy the extras when you can.

✔ **Set spending limits:** This is like creating boundaries for your spending to ensure you stay within your budget and use your money wisely. It's like saying, "I won't spend more than this amount on snacks this month." Setting limits keeps you in control of your spending. When you reach the limit for a category, it's a sign that you need to stop spending on that particular thing for the month.

✔ **Stick to your budget:** Keep track of your spending to ensure you're not exceeding your limits. It's like following the rules of a game to score points and win. Sticking to your spending limits is a great way to learn discipline and ensure your money lasts until the end of the month.

✔ **Adjust when needed:** If you're overspending in one category, you might need to cut back on another. It's like changing your game strategy when you're not winning.

✔ **Prioritize saving:** Don't forget to allocate a portion of your income for saving. Prioritizing your savings is like putting your future first and ensuring you have money set aside for your long-term goals.

✔ **Be tech-savvy:** Explore different methods and tools for setting up and monitoring your budget, including mobile apps like Goodbudget, Money Tracker, and Budget Planner. These apps work like unique gaming gadgets, smoothing your financial journey. They assist you in creating budgets, keeping an eye on your spending, and monitoring your savings.

✔ **Review and reflect:** At the end of the month, look at how well you stuck to your budget. Monitor how much you've spent in each category throughout the month. This is like checking your score in a game. If you're close to reaching the limit, you can decide to save for the next month or adjust your spending in another category.

Creating a budget is like having a strategy guide for your finances. It helps you make the most of your money and reach your goals. So, start budgeting today and level up your money management skills!

9.
Building Healthy Financial Habits: Avoiding Debt and Overspending

Beware of little
expenses;
   a small leak
   will sink
   a great ship.
benjamin franklin

Hey Guy!
Another secret you need to know to have financial freedom is to live within your means and steer clear of borrowing and overspending. Debt means borrowing money, like when you ask for a loan or use a credit card. It might seem like a quick way to get something you want, but it often costs more in the long run. Think of it as a tricky puzzle in a game – it's hard to get out of. Avoiding debt and overspending is like having a shield that protects your money.

Here are some things you need to know and do:

- ✔ **Avoid the debt trap:** Like in a game, you can get trapped in debt if you borrow too much. This means you owe more than you can quickly repay, and escaping can be challenging. Debt can be like a monster that haunts you.

- ✔ **Save first:** Instead of borrowing, save your money. Imagine saving as collecting treasures in a game. The more you save, the richer you become, and you won't need to borrow.

- ✔ **Budget wisely:** Create a budget that guides your spending. Stick to the limits you set so you don't overspend. It's like following a map in a game to reach your destination.

- ✔ **Think before you spend:** Before you buy something, ask yourself if it's a need or a want. Is it necessary, like food or school supplies, or just something you'd like to have, like a new game? If it is not a need and it is not necessary, then don't buy it.

- ✔ **Save for goals:** Plan to save for your goals, like a new phone or a fun trip. Using your own money for these things feels more fabulous than borrowing.

- ✔ **Avoid impulse buys:** Impulse buying is like making quick decisions in a game without thinking them through. Pause and consider your purchases carefully.

- ✔ **Learn from mistakes:** If you overspend or get into debt, don't worry. It's like making a wrong move in a game. Learn from it and try not to repeat the same mistake.

- ✔ **Seek help:** If you're struggling with debt, seek support from a trusted individual, such as a family member. It's like getting advice from a wise mentor in a game.

By avoiding debt and overspending, you're giving yourself the power to control your financial future. It's like winning a game where you make the smart moves to succeed.

10.
Making Your Money Work for You: Investing Strategies for Emerging Giants

Money is only a tool. It will take you wherever you wish, but it will not replace you as the driver.

Greetings, Budding Millionaires!

Do you know that making money work for you is like having a superpower that helps you achieve your dreams? One significant avenue to wield money as a tool for your benefit is through investing. In the following, I'll delve into the essence of investment, various strategies, plans, and the magic of compound interest.

☐ Investing: The Magic of Growing Your Money

Investing means using your money to make more money. It is the key to making your money grow faster. It's like planting seeds that grow into a money tree. When you invest, your money has the potential to increase in value over the years.

Here's how to understand it with simple language:

- ✔ **Planting seeds:** When you invest, it's like planting tiny seeds of money. These seeds have the potential to grow into bigger plants that yield more money. It's similar to how your game character levels up and strengthens.

- ✔ **Time is your ally:** Investing is about patience and giving your money time to grow. Like in a game, the more time you have, your character becomes more powerful. In investing, the more time your money has to grow, the more it can multiply.

- ✔ **Earning rewards:** Over time, your invested money earns rewards, just like completing quests in a game earns you points. These rewards can come in the form of interest, dividends, or an increase in the value of your investments.

- ✔ **The power of compound interest:** Think of compound interest as a game booster. It makes your money grow faster because you earn interest not only on your initial investment but also on the interest you've already earned. It's like gaining extra points with each level you conquer in a game.

✔ **Diversify your plants:** It's wise to diversify instead of putting all your seeds in one plant. This means investing in different things, like stocks, bonds, or real estate. It's like having various skills and equipment in a game to handle multiple challenges.

✔ **Play the long game:** Investing is not a quick win; it's a long game. Be patient and allow your investments to grow over many years. Like in a game, success often comes to those who plan for the long term.

By understanding the magic of investing, you can make your money work for you and grow into a valuable asset over time. It's like watching your game character become more powerful as you progress through the levels. So, start planting your money seeds and watch them become mighty money trees.

❑ **Unlocking Wealth: Simple Investment Strategies for Youths**

Let's explore simple and effective investment strategies to grow your money wisely.

Here are simple strategies to consider:

✔ **Learn the basics:** Imagine investing as a new game. Start by learning the rules. Understand what stocks, bonds, and mutual funds are. Think of them as different game characters, each with strengths and weaknesses.

✔ **Set clear goals:** Like in a game, you need to know your objectives. Are you saving for a big purchase, like a car or college? Or are you aiming to build wealth for your future? Having clear goals helps you stay focused.

✔ **Diversify your investments:** Diversifying is like having a well-rounded team in a game. It means spreading your investments across different options. This lowers your risk, so if one investment isn't doing well, others might be.

✔ **Start small:** You don't need much money to begin. Think of it as starting at a lower level in a game and working your way up. Begin with what you can afford, and as you learn and gain confidence, you can increase your investments.

✔ **Use time to your advantage:** Time is like a superpower in this game. The earlier you start playing (investing), the more levels you can complete, and the stronger your team becomes. Like in your favorite video game, leveling up early helps unlock more abilities and powers. In investing, the longer your money remains invested, the greater its growth potential.

✔ **Stay informed:** Keep an eye on your investments as you would watch for game updates. Imagine you're playing a game, and there are updates and patches that you need to keep track of. Similarly, in the world of investing, you need to stay informed. You watch how your characters (investments) are performing. If some aren't doing well, you make changes to your team to ensure you stay on the path to victory.

✔ **Consult for guidance:** Feel free to seek advice from adults you trust or financial experts. It's like asking for tips from experienced players in a game who can give you valuable tips to improve your strategy. They can provide valuable insights to help you make better investment decisions.

✔ **Be patient:** Investing is a long-term strategy, like working on a quest in a game that takes time to complete. The more patient you are, the more likely you are to see your team (investments) succeed and achieve your goals. So, be patient and allow your investments to grow steadily.

By following these simple strategies, you're on your way to growing your money and leveling up your financial future, just like you do in your favorite games. So, start your investing adventure and watch your money grow!

☐ The Magic of Compound Interest: How Your Money Grows

Hey guys!

Do you know that compound interest is like a magic boost, it makes your money grow faster because you earn interest not only on your initial investment but also on the interest you've already earned. It multiplies your money over time, just like gaining extra points in a game as you advance.

Here are some truths you should know about compound interest:

- ✔ It is free extra money you earn on your savings. It's like a game where you collect bonuses as you play.

- ✔ The longer you save, the more powerful compound interest becomes. It's like levelling up in a game. The more levels you pass, the stronger your character gets.

- ✔ When you save or invest, your money earns interest. With compound interest, the interest you earn is added to your original savings. Then, you earn interest on both your original savings and the interest you've already earned. It's like winning extra points in a game, and those points earn more points!

- ✔ The sooner you start saving, the greater opportunity your money has to grow through compound interest. It's like being ahead in a game because you started playing early.

✔ Just like playing a game regularly helps you improve, adding more money to your savings or investments regularly can make compound interest work even better.

✔ Compound interest is a long-term game. The more patient you are, the more you can benefit from its magic. It's like solving a puzzle in a game that gets easier as you keep playing.

✔ The growth may seem slow at first, like earning small rewards in a game. But over time, the growth becomes significant, and your money multiplies impressively.

Understanding compound interest is like finding a treasure in a game that keeps growing. The longer you keep your money invested, the more you'll see its magical effects. So, start early, be patient, and let compound interest work its charm to help you reach your financial goals.

☐ **Investing Plans for Youngsters: A Guide to Growing Your Money**

There are different ways to invest, just like choosing different game strategies.

Here are some examples of investment plans that you can consider:

✔ **Stocks:** You can invest in individual company stocks. For instance, you could purchase shares of well-known companies like Apple, Amazon, or Microsoft through a brokerage account. When the company does well, the value of your stock can increase. It's a bit like forming alliances in a game to gain more power.

✔ **Savings accounts:** While not considered traditional investments, savings accounts can be a safe place for you to earn interest on your savings. These are like secure vaults in a game where you can store your money, and your money will be safe. Many banks offer savings accounts specifically for youngsters with low or no fees.

✔ **Mutual funds:** When you and other investors pool your money together, a professional manager decides where to invest it. It's like teaming up with other players in a game to win more rewards. Youths can choose mutual funds based on their risk tolerance and investment goals.

✔ **Certificates of deposit (CDs):** CDs are time-based deposits that offer higher interest rates than regular savings accounts. You can invest in CDs with different maturity periods, such as 6 months, 1 year, or more.

✔ **Robo-Advisors:** Robo-advisors are automated investment platforms that create and manage a diversified portfolio for you based on your risk tolerance and goals. You can start investing with relatively small amounts through Robo-advisors.

✔ **Educational investment accounts:** Some parents set up custodial accounts for their children. These accounts can include Uniform Gifts to Minors Act (UGMA) or Uniform Transfers to Minors Act (UTMA) accounts. They allow parents to invest on behalf of their children, and they gain control of the account when they reach a certain age.

✔ **Peer-to-peer lending:** You can explore peer-to-peer lending platforms where you can lend money to individuals or small businesses in exchange for interest payments.

✔ **Real estate investment trusts (REITs):** REITs own, operate, or finance income-producing real estate. You can invest in REITs that expose you to the real estate market without purchasing physical properties.

✔ **Cryptocurrencies:** You may be interested in investing in cryptocurrencies like Bitcoin or Ethereum. However, you should be aware of this asset class's high volatility and risks.

It's essential for young guys like you to research and understand each investment option, consider their financial goals and risk tolerance, and, if necessary, seek guidance from adults or financial experts before making any investments.

11.
Earning Money as a Youngster: Your Guide to Financial Independence

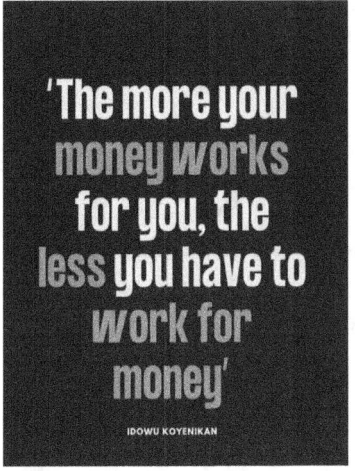

'The more your money works for you, the less you have to work for money'

IDOWU KOYENIKAN

What's Up, Soon-To-Be Millionaires?
Becoming financially independent as a youngster involves exploring various avenues to earn money. Here are some practical ideas to kickstart your journey toward financial independence:

1. Entrepreneurial Opportunities: These are special quests tailored to your unique skills. You can explore your talents in arts, crafts, or any unique skill you have. Turn your passion into a small business, selling handmade items or serving your community. Examples include;

✔ **Small business ventures:** You can start a small business based on your interests and skills. This could involve selling handmade crafts and custom artwork or providing a service like dog walking, tutoring, or lawn care. It's a chance to be your own boss. Identify your strengths and turn them into a business opportunity.

✔ **Online ventures:** The internet provides a vast platform for entrepreneurial youths. You can explore e-commerce by selling products on platforms like Etsy or creating and selling digital products. You can also venture into content creation on platforms like YouTube or blogging.

✔ **Freelancing:** If you have specific skills, such as writing, graphic design, programming, or social media management, you can offer your services on freelance platforms like LinkedIn, Fiverr or Upwork, which will help you connect with people looking for your skills. The platform allows you to work on projects for clients and earn income.

✔ **Event services:** You can offer event planning and coordination services. This could include helping organize birthday parties and small gatherings or providing photography services for local events.

✔ **Local artisanal ventures:** You may choose to explore artisanal ventures by creating and selling unique, handcrafted items. This could include jewelry, clothing, or home decor. Local markets and craft fairs provide opportunities to showcase and sell these products.

✔ **Social media management:** With the prevalence of social media, you can offer social media management services to local businesses. This involves creating and managing content, scheduling posts, and engaging with the audience on behalf of businesses.

✔ **Technology services:** If you have digital skills, you can offer services such as computer troubleshooting, basic coding, or website development for individuals or small businesses in your community.

✔ **Educational services:** If you excel in certain subjects, you can offer tutoring services to younger students in your community. This helps the learner and allows you to monetize your knowledge.

✔ **Environmental services:** Initiatives related to environmental sustainability can be explored. This might include starting a small recycling program, promoting eco-friendly products, or organizing local clean-up events.

✔ **Odd jobs:** Odd jobs are mini-quests you can complete for neighbors or family friends. It could be mowing lawns, walking dogs, or helping with household chores. It's a flexible way to earn money while being helpful in your community.

Entrepreneurial opportunities provide a source of income and foster valuable skills such as creativity, problem-solving, communication, and financial management. It's an avenue to explore your passions, contribute to your community, and gain practical experience in the world of business.

2. Start Part-Time Jobs: Think of part-time jobs as the first level in earning money. It's a great way to earn money and build skills while gaining real-world experience. Examples include;

✔ **Retail jobs:** Cashier, Sales Assistant, and Stock Clerk.

✔ **Food service jobs:** Waiter/Waitress, Host/Hostess, and Dishwasher/Kitchen Assistant.

✔ **Customer service jobs:** Call Center Representative and Customer Service Representative

✔ **Outdoor jobs:** Lifeguard, Golf Caddy, Landscaping Assistant, Event Usher for local events or weddings, Farm Worker during harvest seasons

- ✔ **Office jobs:** Office Assistant and Data Entry Clerk
- ✔ **Tutoring:** Subject Tutor, Language Tutor, and Homework Helper
- ✔ **Pet care jobs:** Dog Walker and Pet Sitter
- ✔ **Entertainment industry jobs:** Movie Theater Attendant and Amusement Park Attendant
- ✔ **Babysitting:** Babysitter and Mother's Helper
- ✔ **Technology jobs:** Computer Lab Assistant, Social Media Assistant, or local influencers.
- ✔ **Fitness jobs:** Fitness Instructor Assistant, Gym Receptionist, and Sports Event Assistant.
- ✔ **Art and creative jobs:** Art Gallery Assistant and Photographer's Assistant.
- ✔ **Delivery jobs:** Newspaper Delivery and Food Delivery Driver.
- ✔ **Summer camp jobs:** Camp Counselor and Program Assistant.
- ✔ **Librarian assistant:** Shelving Books and Assisting with Library Programs.
- ✔ **Local services:** House Cleaning or Home Organization and Car Washing.

✔ **Music lessons assistant:** Assist a local music teacher or offer beginner music lessons

✔ **Gardening assistant:** Assist with gardening and lawn maintenance for residents

Always ensure that any job you consider complies with local labor laws and regulations. Consider your interests, skills, and schedule when looking for a part-time job. It's not just about earning money but also gaining valuable experience and skills that will benefit you in the future.

3. Develop your skills: Developing your skills as a soon-to-be millionaire is an exciting and valuable journey. It is a lifelong process that involves continuous learning, practice, and improvement. Here's a guide to help you navigate this process:

✔ **Self-reflection:**

- Reflect on your interests, passions, hobbies, and areas you'd like to improve.
- Identify areas where you feel a natural inclination or curiosity.
- Identify soft skills (communication, teamwork) and hard skills (coding, graphic design) that align with your goals.

✔ Explore various fields:

- Try out different activities to discover what you enjoy.
- Attend workshops, join clubs, or participate in extracurricular activities.

✔ Set clear goals:

- Define specific, measurable, achievable, relevant, and time-bound (SMART) goals for skill development.
- Break down your goals into smaller, attainable steps.

✔ Create a learning plan:

- Research learning resources such as online courses, books, workshops, and mentors.
- Develop a structured plan to acquire knowledge and practical experience.

✔ Embrace creativity:

- Explore creative outlets like writing, drawing, or music.
- Creativity enhances problem-solving skills and fosters innovation.

✔ **Utilize online learning:**

- Explore online platforms like Coursera, Udemy, Khan Academy, or LinkedIn Learning.
- Take advantage of free and paid courses encompassing diverse subjects to acquire new knowledge or refine existing skills.

✔ **Seek Guidance and Feedback:**

- Reach out to teachers, mentors, or older students for advice.
- Ask questions and seek guidance on potential career paths.
- Actively seek feedback from mentors, peers, or instructors.
- Use constructive feedback to identify areas for improvement and refinement.

✔ **Practice Regularly:**

- Practice is crucial to skill development. Allocate time each day or week to practice what you've learned.
- Apply your skills to real-world projects or challenges.

✔ **Join Communities:**

- Join school clubs, online, or local communities related to your field of interest.
- Pose inquiries, participate in discussions, and draw insights from others' experiences.
- Collaborate with individuals who share similar interests and leverage each other's strengths for mutual learning.
- Connect with classmates and peers who share similar interests.

✔ **Attend Workshops and Conferences:**

- Participate in workshops, conferences, and meetups to connect with professionals in your industry.
- Network with professionals or enthusiasts in fields that interest you.

✔ **Stay Informed:**

- Keep up-to-date with industry trends, advancements, and best practices.
- Read pertinent publications, subscribe to newsletters, and track industry leaders on social media.

- Cultivate a curious mindset by asking questions and seeking answers.
- Stay informed about global issues and emerging trends.

✔ **Build a Portfolio:**

- Document your projects, achievements, and activities.
- Create a portfolio showcasing your work and projects.
- A portfolio is a tangible representation of your skills and can be shared with potential employers or collaborators.

✔ **Stay Persistent and Patient:**

- Skill development takes time and perseverance.
- Celebrate small victories, and understand that improvement is a continuous process.

✔ **Stay Adaptable:**

- Be open to adapting your skills based on feedback and experiences.
- Welcome change and perceive challenges as chances for personal development.

✔ Time Management:

- Learn to manage your time effectively between school, activities, and relaxation.
- Balancing responsibilities prepares you for future challenges.

Remember, skill development is a dynamic process. Enjoy the journey, and don't be afraid to explore different paths. Each experience contributes to your growth and prepares you for future opportunities.

12.
Building a Wealthy Mindset: Your Guide to Financial Empowerment

"If you never dream, you will never know the endless possibilities of what you can become."

—Annette White

Hey there, Young Financial Adventurer!
Welcome to the journey of building a wealthy mindset, which empowers you to achieve financial success and navigate everyday challenges. Let's delve into the key topics that will help shape your perspective for a prosperous future.

☐ **Understanding Your Mindset:**

✔ **Your money mindset**: Understanding your mindset involves recognizing your beliefs and attitudes toward money. Reflect on how you view wealth, success, and financial goals. Identify any limiting beliefs that may hinder your financial growth.

✔ **Positive vibes:** Cultivate a positive mindset that sees opportunities in challenges rather than obstacles and setbacks as stepping stones to success.

☐ **Overcoming Common Financial Challenges:**

✔ **Facing challenges head-on:** Understand that financial challenges are a part of life, and everyone faces money challenges. Learn to face them with resilience.

✔ **Budgeting basics:** Learn the art of budgeting, go may need to go through chapter eight again and master the art. It's like creating a roadmap for your money. It helps you stay on track.

✔ **Smart spending:** Know the difference between needs and wants. Prioritize spending on things that truly matter.

☐ **Staying Motivated and Resilient:**

✔ **Setting goals:** Define clear financial goals. They give purpose to your money decisions.

✔ **Celebrate your achievements:** Acknowledge and celebrate your victories, big or small. It's like acknowledging your progress on this financial adventure.

✔ **Learning from your mistakes and setbacks:** Learning from your failures, embrace setbacks as opportunities to learn and grow. When things don't go as planned, see it as a chance to learn and bounce back stronger.

Building a wealthy mindset isn't just about having money; it's about developing a positive and resilient attitude towards the financial ups and downs life may throw your way. Your mindset is your secret weapon on the path to financial success. With the right mindset, you'll be better equipped to navigate the twists and turns on the pathway to financial success. So, stay positive, stay motivated, and enjoy the process of shaping your wealthy mindset!

13.
Creating Your Financial Vision:
A Brighter Future Awaits

Today is your opportunity to build the tomorrow you want.

—KEN POIROT

Hey, Rising Financial Stars!

Creating a vision for your financial future is like setting your compass to guide you toward your dream life. It's like daydreaming about the amazing things you want to accomplish with your money. Let's explore how to do it:

✔ **Imagine your dreams:** Take some time to daydream about what you want your financial future to look like. Do you see yourself owning a home, traveling the world, or starting a business? Your vision is your chance to dream big.

✔ **Set specific goals:** Turn those dreams into clear financial goals. Instead of saying, "I want to travel," say, "I want to save $2,000 for a trip to Europe next summer." Specific goals make your vision more achievable.

✔ **Prioritize your goals:** Not all goals are equal. Decide which goals are most important to you and deserve your attention first. Maybe your priority is saving for college before anything else.

✔ **Make a plan:** Your vision needs a plan. Think about what steps you need to take to reach your goals. If it's saving, plan how much you'll save each month.

✔ **Stay motivated:** Your vision can keep you motivated. When you see your dreams becoming a reality, it's like a boost of energy to keep working towards your financial goals.

✔ **Adjust as you grow:** Your vision might change as you grow and experience new things. That's okay! Your vision is meant to evolve with you.

Remember, creating a vision for your financial future is all about shaping the life you want. It's like drawing a map to reach your dreams. Your financial adventure is just beginning, and you're the artist creating your masterpiece!

Tracking Your Progress: Navigating Your Financial Journey

Tracking your progress is like having a map while on an adventure. It helps you see how far you've come and what's left to explore. Let's talk about how you can track your financial journey:

✔ **Keep a record:** Think of this as your financial journal. Keep track of your money coming in, like earnings, financial gifts, allowances, money spent on clothes, gadgets like smartphones, tablets, and laptops, money for buying gifts for friends and family, games, and snacks. This record will show you where your money is flowing.

✔ **Set milestones:** Imagine your financial journey as a series of checkpoints. Set milestones for your goals, such as saving a specific amount. For example, if your goal is to save $100, celebrate when you've saved $25, $50, and so on.

✔ **Use tools:** Utilize helpful apps and tools to make tracking of your money easier. Apps like Goodbudget, Money Tracker, Budget planner and others. They act like special gadgets in a game, making your journey smoother. You can use them to create budgets, track your spending, and monitor your savings.

✔ **Reflect and adjust:** Just like in a game, take time to reflect on your progress. Are you getting closer to your goals? If not, it's okay. You can adjust your plan and try different approaches to improve your financial game.

✔ **Stay Motivated:** Tracking your progress is like watching your score rise in a game. It's exciting and motivating! Celebrate your accomplishments, even the small ones. It keeps you focused and eager to achieve your financial goals.

✔ **Learn from mistakes:** Sometimes, you make mistakes and learn from them in games. It's the same with money. If you overspend one month, learn from it and adjust for the next month. Think of it as leveling up your financial skills.

✔ **Share with friends:** Just like sharing your game achievements with friends, share your financial goals and progress with friends or family who can support and encourage you on your financial journey.

Tracking your financial progress is like having a GPS for your money adventure. It helps you stay on the right path toward your goals. Remember, it's your financial journey, and you're the captain steering it to success!

14.

Taking Action: Steps to Start Your Journey to Wealth

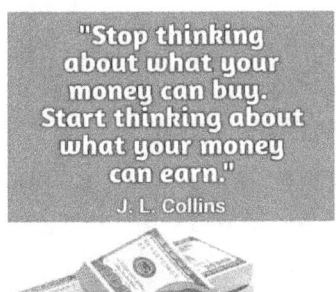

"Stop thinking about what your money can buy. Start thinking about what your money can earn."

J. L. Collins

Hey, Future Financial Superhero!

Ready to take charge of your money? Let's break down the steps to kickstart your journey to wealth:

Dream Big: It's time to dream big because your dreams are the blueprint for your financial adventure. Here's how to let your imagination soar:

✔ **Define your goals:** Picture the Future, close your eyes, and envision your ideal life. What does it look like? Where are you? What are you doing? Split your dreams into short-term (the next year or two) and long-term (five years and beyond) goals. Set and clarify your goals

✔ **Be specific:** Precision is crucial; the more specific, the better. If you dream of traveling, where exactly do you want to go? What experiences do you want to have?

✔ **Financial freedom:** What would financial freedom look like for you? Being debt-free, having savings, or having the freedom to choose your career path?

✔ **Explore passions:** Follow Your Heart. What are you passionate about? Your dream could involve turning your passion into a business or career.

✔ **Visualize success:** Create a Vision Board. Cut out pictures or words from magazines that represent your goals. Stick them on a board and put them where you can see them daily.

✔ **Express your aspirations:** Discuss your dreams with a trusted friend, family member, or mentor. Saying them out loud makes them more real.

✔ **Stay open-minded:** Evolve your dreams as you grow. Your dreams may change. Stay open to new possibilities and be ready to adjust your goals.

✔ **Believe in yourself:** Believe that your dreams are achievable, believe you can do it, and you have the power to turn your dreams into reality.

Remember, dreaming big is like creating the map for your financial journey. Your dreams guide your goals, and your goals guide your actions. So, dream big, aim high, and get ready to unleash your financial superpowers!

Budget Like a Boss: Ready to take control of your cash? It's time to budget like a boss. Here's your guide to mastering your money moves:

✔ **Know your money:** Figure out how much you have coming in (income from a part-time job, allowance, or gigs) and your expenses (everything you spend money on).

✔ **Create a budget:** Set spending limits. Decide how much you'll spend in each category—like food, entertainment, and savings. Prioritize your savings by saving money at the top of your budget. Treat it like a superhero mission—you're saving the day!

✔ **Track your spending:** Stay accountable by recording every purchase. There are fantastic apps like Goodbudget or Money Tracker to help you stay on top of your spending game.

✔ **Emergency fund magic:** Save some money for unexpected expenses. It's like having a superhero fund for emergencies.

✔ **Be a smart shopper:** Compare prices before buying things. Check if you can get a better deal. Superheroes always find the best value for their money. Avoid impulse buys. Think before you buy. Do you really need it, or is it just a momentary desire?

✔ **Adjust and adapt:** Your budget isn't set in stone, so review regularly. Check it periodically and adjust if needed. Life changes, and so can your budget.

✔ **Make saving a habit:** Every time you get money, put a portion into savings. It's the superhero way to build wealth. When you hit your savings goals, celebrate! You're one step closer to financial superhero status.

Budgeting like a boss is your secret weapon to financial freedom. It's not about restricting yourself but about being in control and making your money work for you. So, suit up, superhero—your budget awaits!

Unlocking the Secrets of Investing: Ready to unravel the mysteries of investing? Let's dive into the basics and understand how to make your money work for you:

✔ **Decoding the investing language:** Explore the different investment choices such as stocks, bonds, mutual funds, and ETFs. It's like learning a new language; each investment type has its unique dialect.

✔ **Utilize the power of compound interest:** Take advantage of the magic of compound interest. The longer your money stays invested, the more it multiplies. It's like planting seeds that grow into a financial forest over time.

✔ **Avoid debt traps:** Be a superhero saver, not a debt collector. Say no to unnecessary debts and yes to smart saving.

✔ **Understand the concept of risk and reward:** Every investment involves a trade-off between potential gains and possible losses. It's like finding the right balance on a seesaw.

✔ **Diversification:** Don't put all your eggs in one basket; learn the importance of diversification. It's like having a variety of superpowers in your financial arsenal to protect against unexpected challenges.

✔ **Setting investment goals:** Define your objectives and clarify your investment goals. Whether saving for a big purchase or growing your wealth over time, knowing your dreams is like having a treasure map for your financial journey.

✔ **Learn from investment legends:** Study the strategies of successful investors like Warren Buffett, Peter Lynch, Benjamin Graham and others. It's like taking lessons from financial legends who have mastered the art of investing.

✔ **Explore the buy-and-hold strategy:** It's like collecting rare items in a video game and watching their value increase over time.

✔ **Stay informed:** Keep yourself informed about market trends and economic news. Knowing the financial landscape is like having a radar to navigate your investment journey.

✔ **Start small, think big:** Begin with small investments. It's like practicing your skills in a video game—you start with the easy levels before tackling the big challenges.

✔ **Seek guidance:** Stay connected, and don't hesitate to seek advice from experienced investors and mentors who can share their wealth-building wisdom. It's like having a wise wizard guide you through the enchanted forest of investments.

✔ **Begin early:** Time is Your Superpower; the earlier you start your money mission, the more time your money has to grow. Starting early empowers you to make the most of your money. So, embrace your financial superpowers, and let the early adventure begin!

✔ **Stay super motivated:** Keep your eyes on the prize. Wealth-building is a journey with ups and downs. Stay motivated by remembering your goals. Celebrate your achievements along the way.

Understanding investing is like learning the rules of a thrilling game. So, gear up, future investor! Your journey into the world of investments is about to begin.

15.

Frequently Asked Questions and Answers about Your Journey to Wealth-Building

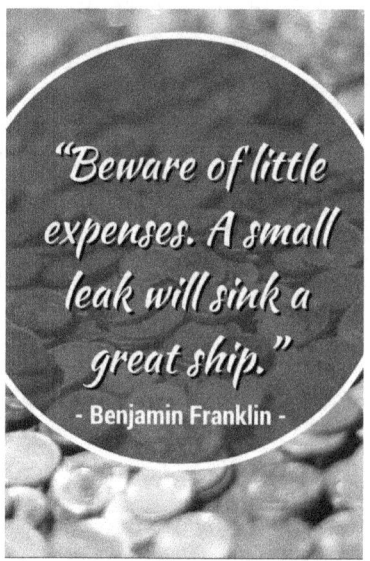

"Beware of little expenses. A small leak will sink a great ship."
- Benjamin Franklin -

Hey Young Wealth-Builders!
Let's dive into some common questions you might have on your journey to financial success:

1. What is Wealth, anyway?
   Answer: Wealth is more than just money; it's the ability to live on your terms. It includes financial security, the freedom to choose, and the power to pursue your dreams.
2. Why Should I Start Learning About Money Now?

Answer: The earlier you start, the more time your money has to grow. Learning now sets you up for a future where you have the knowledge and habits to make smart financial decisions.

3. What's the Importance of Setting Financial Goals?

   Answer: Goals give your money a purpose. Whether saving for a dream trip or starting a business, setting financial goals helps you stay focused and motivated.

4. How Can I Build a Strong Foundation for Wealth?

   Answer: Understand the basics of money, avoid common misconceptions, prioritize financial education, and embrace the power of early financial literacy.

5. Should I Save Money Even If I Don't Have Much?

   Answer: Absolutely! No matter how small, every bit you save adds up over time. It's not about the amount but the habit of saving that contributes to your financial well-being.

6. How Can I Avoid Overspending and Debts?

   Answer: Make a budget, prioritize needs over wants, resist the urge to borrow for unnecessary things, and be mindful of your spending habits.

7. What's the Secret to Building Wealth as a Youth?

   Answer: There's no secret—just a combination of learning early, saving consistently, avoiding unnecessary debts, and making informed financial decisions.

8. How Can I Understand Wealth and Financial Well-being?

   Answer: Learn the basics of money, budgeting, and the role of financial education. Understanding these concepts is like building the foundation of a strong financial house.

9. Are There Common Misconceptions About Wealth?

   Answer: Yes! Some think savings can wait, but starting early is crucial. Also, avoid the misconception that a higher income means you can't start saving now.

10. Is Building Wealth Just About Having a Lot of Money?

    Answer: No, it's about making smart financial choices, saving consistently, and understanding the value of money.

11. How Can I Avoid Common Pitfalls in My Financial Journey?

    Answer: Be aware of common misconceptions, prioritize financial education, and stay disciplined in your money habits.

12. Can I Build Wealth Even If I Need to Earn More?

    Answer: Absolutely! Wealth-building is about habits. Start saving, avoid unnecessary debts, and make informed financial choices.

13. What Exactly is Financial Education?
   Answer: Financial education is the knowledge and skills needed to make informed and effective decisions about money. It's your guide to mastering the art of personal finance.
14. Why is Financial Education a Superpower?
   Answer: It empowers you to take control of your financial future, make smart decisions, and confidently navigate the complex world of money.
15. How Does Financial Education Put You in Control?
   Answer: It equips you with the tools to budget wisely, save effectively, invest intelligently, and avoid common financial pitfalls.
16. Can I Learn About Finance Even If I need to improve in Math?
   Answer: Absolutely! Financial education is about practical knowledge and decision-making. You can be something other than a math genius to understand and apply it.
17. Is Financial Education Only About Budgeting?
   Answer: No, it covers a broad spectrum—from budgeting and saving to investing, understanding credit, and making informed financial decisions in various life situations.
18. Can Financial Education Help Avoid Common Money Mistakes?

Answer: Absolutely! It teaches you to recognize and avoid common pitfalls, ensuring a smoother financial journey.

19. How Can I Make Financial Education Fun?

    Answer: Explore interactive apps, games, and real-life scenarios. Learning about money doesn't have to be boring—it can be an exciting adventure!

20. Can Healthy Financial Habits Help Avoid Money Stress?

    Answer: Absolutely! Establishing good habits reduces stress by creating a stable financial foundation.

21. How Can I Start Building Healthy Money Habits?

    Answer: Start small—create a budget, save consistently, and make mindful spending choices. It's like training for a financial marathon.

22. Is It Too Early to Start Building Habits as a Youth?

    Answer: Not at all! The earlier you start, the more ingrained these habits become. It's like planting seeds for a money-savvy future.

23. What's the Role of Budgeting in Healthy Financial Habits?

    Answer: Budgeting is like your financial GPS—it helps you navigate your spending savings and ensures you stay on the right track.

24. How Can I Avoid Overspending and Impulse Purchases?

Answer: Set spending limits, differentiate between needs and wants, and think twice before making impulse buys. It's about making intentional choices.

25. Can Healthy Financial Habits Help Reach Financial Goals?

    Answer: Absolutely! Healthy habits align your daily choices with your long-term goals, making it easier to achieve them.

26. Why is Tracking Spending Important in Building Healthy Habits?

    Answer: Tracking spending keeps you accountable, helps identify patterns, and ensures you stay within your budget. It's like keeping score in a game.

27. How Can I Stay Motivated in Building Healthy Financial Habits?

    Answer: Celebrate small victories, visualize your financial goals, and surround yourself with positive influences. It's about staying motivated on your money journey.

28. Why Should Youths Consider Investing?

    Answer: Investing allows your money to grow over time, providing financial security and opportunities for the future.

29. What's the Difference Between Saving and Investing?

    Answer: Saving is preserving money while investing involves putting money into assets to generate returns. Investing carries more risk but offers greater potential rewards.

30. How Can I Learn About Different Investment Options?

Answer: Explore resources, attend workshops, and consider seeking advice from experienced investors or financial experts. Knowledge is your best asset.

31. Are There Risks Involved in Investing?
    Answer: Investing carries risks, but understanding and managing those risks is part of becoming a savvy investor. Diversification and research are essential.

32. What's the Role of Compound Interest in Investing?
    Answer: Compound interest is like magic for investors. It allows your money to earn interest on both the initial principal and the accumulated interest, leading to accelerated growth.

33. How Can Youths Develop Their Own Investing Strategies?
    Answer: Start by setting clear financial goals, understanding risk tolerance, and diversifying your investments. Continuously educate yourself and adapt your strategy as needed.

34. Is It Possible to Recover from Investment Mistakes?
    Answer: Yes, mistakes happen. The key is to learn from them. Consider them as valuable lessons that contribute to your growth as an investor.

35. Can Youths Make a Positive Impact Through Ethical Investing?
    Answer: Absolutely! Ethical or socially responsible investing allows you to support

causes you believe in while growing your wealth.

36. Why Should Youths Start Earning Money?

Answer: Earning money as a youth teaches valuable life skills, fosters independence, and sets the stage for financial responsibility.

37. What Are Part-Time Job Options for Youths?

Answer: Youths can explore opportunities like babysitting, tutoring, retail jobs, or working at local businesses. It's a chance to gain experience and earn income.

38. Can Youths Explore Entrepreneurial Opportunities?

Answer: Absolutely! Youths can start small businesses, offer lawn care or pet sitting services, or explore creative ventures online.

39. How Can Youths Start a Small Business?

Answer: Identify your skills or passions, create a business plan, and start small. Whether crafting, tutoring, or tech services, turning hobbies into businesses is a great way to earn.

40. Can Youths Achieve Financial Independence Through Entrepreneurship?

Answer: Yes, entrepreneurship provides a path to financial independence. Building a business allows you to generate income and pursue your passions.

41. What Exactly is a Wealthy Mindset?

Answer: A wealthy mindset involves adopting positive attitudes and beliefs about money, abundance, and one's ability to achieve financial success.

42. How Does Mindset Affect Financial Success?

Answer: Your mindset shapes your actions. A positive and empowered mindset influences financial decisions and opens doors to opportunities.

43. Can Anyone Develop a Wealthy Mindset, Regardless of Their Current Situation?

Answer: Absolutely! Regardless of your current circumstances, developing a wealthy mindset is about changing your perspective and believing in your ability to create financial success.

44. What Role Does Mindset Play in Overcoming Financial Challenges?

Answer: A wealthy mindset helps you view challenges as opportunities for growth. It encourages resilience and creativity in finding solutions.

45. How Can Youths Overcome Common Financial Challenges with a Wealthy Mindset?

Answer: By reframing challenges as learning experiences, setting realistic goals, and staying focused on the long-term benefits of financial empowerment.

46. How Can Youths Stay Resilient in the Face of Financial Setbacks?

Answer: Resilience is a key component of a wealthy mindset. Learn from setbacks, adjust your approach, and keep moving forward with determination.

47. Can Youths Inspire Others by Cultivating a Wealthy Mindset?

Answer: Definitely! Your positive mindset can inspire friends, family, and community to adopt healthier financial attitudes and habits.

48. Why is Taking Action Important in Building Wealth?

Answer: Taking action turns dreams into reality. It's the crucial step that transforms financial goals into achievable milestones.

49. Is It Important for Youths to Stay Consistent in Their Wealth-Building Actions?

Answer: Consistency is key! Regularly review and adjust your plan, stay committed to your goals, and celebrate small wins.

50. How Can Youths Overcome Procrastination and Take Action Today?

Answer: Break tasks into smaller, manageable steps, set deadlines for yourself, and visualize the positive outcomes of taking action.

References

Bowe, F. (2023). *Money Skills for Teens: A Beginner's Guide to Budgeting, Saving, and Investing.* Bemberton. https://www.amazon.com/Money-Skills-Teens-Investing-Everything/dp/1915833086#detailBullets_feature_div

Emmanuel, O. (2011). *Pathway to Wealth.* Common Sense Publishing

Hill, A. (2023). 10 SMART Financial Goals to Build Wealth. https://marriagekidsandmoney.com/smart-financial-goals-to-build-wealth/

Keane, R. (2023). *Financial Literacy for Young Adults Simplified.* Independently published. https://www.amazon.com/Financial-Literacy-Young-Adults-Simplified/dp/B0C9SHJZS9/ref

Lainiotis, G. I. (2023). *Personal Finance for Teens and Young Adults.* Independently published https://www.amazon.com/dp/B0CLB825XH/ref

Lazar, A. (2023). How to Set S.M.A.R.T. Financial Goals (With Examples). Finmasters. https://finmasters.com/smart-financial-goals/#gref

Max, C. (2023). *A smart guide to building wealth blueprint.* Independently published. https://www.amazon.com/smart-guide-building-wealth blueprint/dp/B0C5KNF2Q8#detailBullets_feature_div

Quaye, G. (2023). Personal finance strategies for building wealth: A roadmap to financial success. https://thebftonline.com/2023/08/01/personal-finance-strategies-for-building-wealth-a-roadmap-to-financial-success/

Index